bodymatters

alex does
drugs
Janine amos

CHERRYTREE BOOKS

bodymatters

Kate Smokes Cigarettes
Jon Drinks Alcohol
Why Won't Kim Eat?
Is Helen Pregnant?
Alex Does Drugs
Jamal is Overweight

A Cherrytree Book

First published 2002
by Cherrytree Press
327 High Street
Slough
Berkshire
SL1 1TX

© Evans Brothers Limited 2002

British Library Cataloguing in Publication Data

Amos, Janine
Alex does drugs. - (Bodymatters)
1. Drug abuse - Juvenile literature 2. Drugs -
Physiological effect - Juvenile literature
I. Title
362.2'9

ISBN 1842341103

Printed in Hong Kong by Wing King Tong Co Ltd

Acknowledgements
Planning and production: Discovery Books
Editor: Patience Coster
Photographer: David Simson
Designer: Keith Williams
Artwork: Fred van Deelen
Consultant: Dr Gillian Rice

**All the characters appearing in this book
are played by models.**

Picture acknowledgements
The publisher would like to thank
the following for permission to
reproduce their pictures: Corbis 17;
Impact 23 (Rupert Conant);
Redferns 26 (Simon King).

alex does
drugs

contents

Alex's dad is in a temper.

'Another bad school report!' he shouts at Alex. 'You don't spend half enough time on your homework. You're always out and about. I won't have it! Why can't you be like your brother? We don't have any trouble with Nathan!'

Alex listens in silence. When his dad has finished, Alex slips away. He grabs his skateboard, clicks the front door shut behind him and races down the street, grinning. As soon as he gets to the park he spots Nathan talking with a boy and a girl Alex has never seen before. He balances on his skateboard and glides towards them.

The new boy and girl are called Lee and Sara. They are acting strangely, staggering about and giggling. At first Alex thinks they're drunk. Then Sara sits down and takes a plastic bag out of her pocket, holds it over her nose and breathes in.

'They're sniffing glue,' Nathan whispers.

what are

Sara holds out the bag. 'Are you up for it?' she asks.

Alex isn't sure, but he thinks Sara looks cool.

'OK,' he nods.

'Don't!' warns Nathan. 'Drugs are dangerous.'

'Glue isn't a drug

Chemical effects

Drugs are chemicals that change the way your body and mind work. Drugs are either made in laboratories or occur naturally in plants or minerals. Some drugs are prescribed by doctors as medicines, others are used by people just for pleasure. Many people don't think of glue as a drug, because it was never meant to be used in this way. But Nathan is right – some glues give off strong fumes, called vapours. If these vapours are inhaled, or breathed in, they produce mind-changing effects.

drugs?

ays Alex. 'It'll be a laugh!' He holds out his hand for the bag.

Many people use drugs in their everyday lives. They may take aspirin or paracetamol for a pain or a headache. They may use alcohol or nicotine to give themselves feelings of pleasure. Some drugs, such as cocaine and heroin, are illegal.

Legal drugs (e.g. alcohol, nicotine, penicillin)

Illegal drugs (e.g. heroin, cocaine, cannabis)

When Alex sniffs from the bag there's a strong smell.

Soon he feels light-headed, as if he's floating. He staggers around until he falls over, laughing. Nathan walks away. Alex tries to call him back but he can't get the words out properly.

Alex feels sick and sleepy. Much later, he gets himself home and into bed. He thinks about his school work still lying on the kitchen table.

'Dad'll go mad,' he groans, and then he falls fast asleep.

What are inhalants? Chemicals that are breathed in to give mind-changing effects are called inhalants. There are hundreds of possible inhalants found in homes, schools and offices. Most are poisons.

sniffing glue

Harmful effects

The vapours in the glue contain poisonous chemicals. When Alex breathes in, these pass to his lungs. They are taken into his blood and travel straight to his brain. Alex gets an immediate and powerful feeling of well-being. His heart rate speeds up and he breathes faster.

At the same time, the chemicals are switching off cells in the part of his brain that controls sensible thinking, memory and speech. They travel to the part of his brain concerned with balance too. Alex has difficulty walking. Although Alex may feel lively and excited, the chemicals are actually slowing down the way his brain works.

The main effects of the glue wear off after about half an hour. But some of the chemicals will stay in Alex's brain and nerves for a long time.

People can die the very first time they use an inhalant.

One out of every three people who die from sniffing glue is inhaling for the first time.

DANGER!
People who have been sniffing may:
- suddenly become angry and aggressive
- believe they can do anything – climb high buildings, walk in traffic, leap out of windows
- see and hear things that aren't there
- be sick and choke to death
- die of heart failure

7

Alex meets Lee and Sara most nights after school. Sometimes Nathan is there too with their friend, Mina.

Usually they just hang around. Sometimes they end up sniffing glue or aerosols, but Mina and Nathan don't join in.

One evening Nathan and Alex arrive early. 'I don't understand why you keep sniffing that stuff,' says Nathan. 'It smells horrible. And it makes you act so stupid!'

'Life's boring, that's why!' Alex snaps. 'Boring school and boring homework. And being told off by our boring dad!'

'It's the school play soon,' Nathan continues. 'Why don't you try for a part? It's better than wasting your time with glue.'

Just then they see Lee stumbling towards them. Alex knows that Lee inhales a lot on his own. He's been doing it for years. He's got all kinds of glues and sprays hidden in his dad's garage. He's dirty, his hair is greasy and there are spots all around his mouth. He shakes as he walks.

'Don't let yourself

Lee has built up a tolerance to the chemicals he inhales. This means he needs to inhale more to get the same effect. He's so used to the inhalants fogging his mind, that real life seems scary without them. He feels he needs to sniff chemicals just to get through his day.

Something else is going on in Lee's body too. Over the years, some of the chemicals Lee has inhaled have begun to break down the protective cover that surrounds his nerves. If this cover is broken, the nerve cells will die. Sniffing glue is damaging Lee's brain.

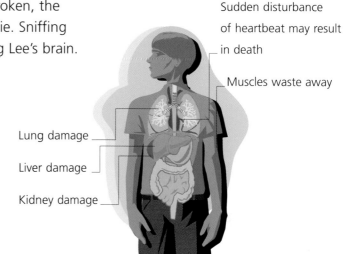

Sudden disturbance of heartbeat may result in death

Muscles waste away

Lung damage

Liver damage

Kidney damage

The damage inhalants can do to the body.

developing a dependency

Many inhalants gradually eat away the protective cover that surrounds brain cells

Damage here can cause loss of memory

This part of the brain controls balance – damage here can cause shaking and clumsy movement

Damage here can cause sight disorders, even blindness

Damage here can cause personality changes and learning problems

Damage from inhalants can slow down or completely stop activity in some parts of the brain.

get like that, Alex,' whispers Nathan.

What is cannabis?

Cannabis comes from a plant. There are three kinds of cannabis.
- the herbal kind, called marijuana, grass or dope, is made from the dried leaves, stalks and seeds of the plant
- cannabis resin, made from a sticky liquid in the plant, comes in blocks
- cannabis oil, the strongest form of the drug

One Friday evening a few weeks later, Alex is very excited.

He's got a part in the play!

'It was cool,' he tells the others. 'Mr Hughes says I'm a born actor!'

'What does your dad say?' asks Mina. 'I thought he wanted you to spend more time on school work?'

'He doesn't know,' says Alex, kicking at a stone.

'Time to celebrate,' says Lee mysteriously. He takes a long cigarette from his pocket and carefully lights it. There's a strange, sweet smell. Alex knows it's cannabis.

Lee takes a deep puff and passes it to Alex. Everyone watches as Alex copies him. At first the smoke makes Alex cough and his eyes water. Soon he relaxes. His worries about his dad fade away. Alex smiles at everyone and he can't stop talking.

Some time later, Nathan shakes Alex's arm. 'Are you listening? It's late. We're going.'

Alex just giggles.

smoking cannabis

Alex is smoking a 'joint' or a 'spliff' – a cigarette containing tobacco and a drug called cannabis.

Highs and lows
Cannabis doesn't always make you chatty and friendly. It often magnifies the way a person feels at the time. Someone who is worried or depressed may become quiet and anxious after smoking. They may get so frightened and panicky that they can hardly move or speak. Sometimes cannabis makes people see or hear things that aren't real. That can be scary.

As Alex smokes the joint, the cannabis affects different parts of his brain.

Memory

Balance and movement

Feelings and emotions

Senses of touch, sight, hearing, taste and smell

Cannabis is a hallucinogen. It changes the way people see and hear things. Cannabis contains many chemicals. One of these, THC, is the main cause of the changes in Alex's mind and body.

When Alex breathes the smoke deep into his lungs, the THC reaches his brain in minutes. Here it sets off a chain of reactions and Alex gets a dreamy, calm, pleasant feeling called a 'high'. THC changes the brain messages that control Alex's senses, feelings and emotions, his memory and judgement. He seems to hear more clearly, see colours more brightly, be more aware of taste and touch. He's charming, friendly and has a lot to say. Everything seems funny. THC also interrupts the working of the part of his brain governing balance and movement. His whole body has loosened up. The effects from the cannabis will last about an hour.

Alex likes the way the cannabis makes him feel.

Over the weeks, he smokes more and more often. Soon he's smoking a joint every evening after school and two or three at weekends. Nothing much seems to worry Alex these days. He often forgets to do his homework. He's never on time. Sometimes he doesn't seem interested in anything. Mina and Nathan are often angry with him.

'We never get any sense out of you now!' Mina shouts one day when Alex doesn't answer her.

'Yeah, he's always stoned, that's why,' says Nathan.

Lee's angry with Alex for a different reason. 'You're smoking all my dope!' he complains.

'I'll take you to see Jim. You can buy your own from now on.'

Many people who try cannabis use it only a few times. Others, like Alex, want it more often. It becomes a habit. People who take cannabis for a long time can come to feel they can't enjoy life without it. They also risk panic attacks and confusion, and they may be unable to remember information they learned seconds ago. They may also experience breathing problems and chest pains. Long-term use can result in lung cancer from the mix of tobacco and cannabis smoke.

Who makes money from drugs?
Jim is a drug dealer. He sells drugs to anyone who will buy them. But he is only one person in a chain of people who make money from drugs. Because the drugs Jim sells are illegal, they have to be smuggled into the country. Police and customs officers spend vast amounts of time and money trying to stop this. Drug smuggling is big business. Huge international organisations transport illegal drugs from one country to another, using up-to-the-minute technology and modern weapons. The people who run these organisations are very wealthy and powerful. Profits from drug smuggling are enormous and many of those involved will bribe or kill to protect their trade.

damage from dope

On Saturday, Alex, Mina and Nathan are in town together.

It's market day and Mina wants to do some shopping. Alex is trying to learn his part in the play. He says his lines over and over, and the others test him.

Later on, they see Sara and Lee among the crowd. Jim is with them. They stay and chat for a while, then Jim pulls out a few white tablets.

'Who wants some fun?' he asks. Nathan and Mina shake their heads.

'It's only E,' laughs Jim. 'Makes you feel really good!'

'It's ecstasy,' says Mina. 'Everyone knows that can kill people!'

'It hasn't killed me,' smiles Lee, taking a tablet.

Alex is not sure. He's scared to try it – but he's curious too. And he doesn't want to look stupid. At last he puts a tablet in his mouth.

Nothing happens for a while. Alex sits with the others while Jim and Lee wander off. Slowly, Alex gets a warm, tingly feeling. He's full of energy and feels like dancing. He smiles round at everyone, strangers too.

ecstasy

DANGER!

Ecstasy can cause:

- panic attacks and confusion
- kidney and liver damage
- brain damage
- people to drink too much water too fast – their brains swell and this can kill them
- people to over-heat and dry out

The ecstasy tablet dissolves in Alex's stomach and passes into his blood. In about 30 minutes it begins to take effect. The drug is a stimulant – it switches on activity in the brain. Ecstasy causes brain chemicals to be released which change Alex's mood. He becomes friendly and full of love. Ecstasy is also a hallucinogen, like cannabis, and once again for Alex the world becomes light, bright and unreal.

The ecstasy in Alex's body has some other effects too. It interferes with his brain's temperature control and his body heat shoots up. His mouth is dry, he's sweating and very, very thirsty.

Mina's right.
People can die from taking
just one ecstasy tablet.

He's tired, fed-up and he's running out of dope. He decides to visit the café where Jim hangs out.

Inside the café, Jim is sitting at a dirty table in the corner. He looks half asleep, but when Alex speaks to him he lifts his head. Alex sits down opposite Jim and quietly asks for what he wants.

'Meet me back here in a couple of hours,' murmurs Jim.

Later that evening, Jim passes Alex a little block of cannabis resin and three ecstasy tablets. And Alex hands Jim the last of the money he's saved from his birthday.

'I can get you some stronger stuff if yo

Cravings

Taking drugs can become a habit for some people. They grow to depend on the drug just to cope with normal life. Sometimes they become addicted, which means they have got so used to the drug that their minds and bodies are unable to do without it. If they don't take the drug, they begin to have a craving (powerful longing) for it. Everything else in life seems unimportant. Some drugs, like crack cocaine or heroin, are known to be powerfully addictive.

16

DANGER!
Heroin can cause:
- mental health problems and depression
- breathing problems
- death from an overdose (accidentally taking too much, too quickly)
- unexplained death
- serious infections (from the use of dirty needles)

drug
addiction

'...want,' says Jim.

Other addictive drugs:
Heroin

Heroin is made from morphine, a chemical found in a plant called the opium poppy. Heroin is a narcotic, a type of drug that relieves pain and makes the person taking it very sleepy. Heroin also affects the brain's 'pleasure pathways' and gives a rush of good feelings. It makes users feel calm and free from worry.

Crack

Crack is a smokeable form of the drug cocaine. It gives a powerful 'high' which may only last about ten minutes. People who smoke a lot of crack may take heroin to blunt their craving for crack.

DANGER!
Crack can cause:
- serious harm to your lungs
- aggressive behaviour and mental health problems
- death from an overdose

Using crack can also lead to heart problems, which may kill.

A few weeks later there's a party. Lots of people from school are there.

It's hot and noisy and very crowded. Alex joins in the dancing. Then he remembers the ecstasy tablets in his pocket. He takes them out and offers one to Mina and Nathan.

'We're having a good time. We don't need drugs!' Mina shouts over the music.

But Alex puts a tablet into his mouth.

Half an hour later, things start to go badly wrong for Alex. He gets the rush of good feelings and the urge to jump for joy that the drug gave him last time. Then, in seconds, bad thoughts start to fill his brain. He feels useless, sad and lonely. He thinks everyone hates him. He hates himself. He goes into the bedroom and lies on the floor. His heart is racing, he's thirsty and he feels sick. Alex starts panting. He thinks he's dying. He's really afraid.

Mina and Nathan find Alex and try to talk to him.

'We can't leave him,' says Nathan. 'Let's give him some juice and take him outside.'

The bad trip scares Alex. He'll never

Mina and Nathan are sensible. Alex needs a quiet place away from lights and music, and he shouldn't be left alone. Alex is having a bad experience caused by the drug he's taken. It's called a bad trip.

The ecstasy in Alex's brain has drained it of a chemical called serotonin, which controls how happy he feels. He's having lots of black thoughts.

Alex is panting because he feels so anxious. As he pants, he breathes out too much of a gas called carbon dioxide. This may cause him to feel dizzy and faint.

A bad trip can happen with any illegal drug. It can happen to anyone, no matter how many times they have taken the drug before. It might be a week before Alex feels completely well again. And the horrors of his trip may come back to him as flashbacks months later.

a bad trip

What's in a drug?
There is no way of checking exactly what an illegal drug contains. Ecstasy tablets are often 'cut' or mixed with something like talcum powder, dog-worming pills or other drugs.

19

.ake ecstasy again.

As the performance of the school play draws nearer, Alex smokes more and more cannabis.

He thinks he can't do without it. And he's always running out of money.

'I need a joint to calm my nerves,' he tells Nathan before a rehearsal. 'Go on, lend me some cash, just until the weekend,' he pleads.

'No way!' says Nathan. 'You owe me loads already.'

Later on, while his dad's in the shower, Alex creeps into the kitchen. He finds his dad's wallet in the dresser. He takes out two notes. Alex knows it's stealing. He feels awful.

On Friday evening there's a big rehearsal. Alex smokes two joints before he arrives. He feels giggly and slow. He forgets his lines. The rehearsal is a disaster.

Afterwards Mr Hughes comes storming across to where Alex is slumped in a chair. The teacher is furious.

'One more stunt like that and you're out of the play!' he shouts.

Everyone's staring

the real cost of drugs

Drug taking is an expensive habit. Alex believes he needs cannabis, so he spends all his pocket money on it. He even steals from his dad to buy the drug.

Very addictive drugs like heroin and crack can cost more. As their bodies become used to the drugs, addicts need to take larger and larger doses to get the same effects.

Drug addicts can spend hundreds of pounds a week on their habit. They can become involved in drug dealing and other crimes to raise the money for their next fix.

Drugs cloud people's judgement and cause them to take risks. Drug users can become violent, cause car accidents, spread disease with infected needles and have unsafe sex. Drug addiction changes people's lives. As well as ruining their health, drugs can cause people to break the law and lose their homes, jobs, families and friends.

t Alex as he stumbles towards the door.

21

22

In school the next day, Mr Hughes speaks to Alex. The teacher looks him straight in the eye.

'I don't know what's going on with you at the moment,' Mr Hughes tells him. 'You're not concentrating. I'll give you one more chance. If you don't change your attitude, I'll be in touch with your father.'

Alex wanders home slowly. 'What am I going to do if Dad finds out I've been nicking money too?' he thinks. 'My friends are fed up with me and I'm messing everything up at school. Drugs are wrecking my life.' It seems to Alex that this is his last chance to make things OK. If he doesn't get a grip now, things will just grow worse. He has to give up drugs.

At first Alex finds it hard to do without cannabis. He gets scared before school every morning. He thinks everyone's looking at him. He worries a lot. Some nights he lies awake for hours, trying to get to sleep.

Alex stops going to the park with the others. He keeps himself busy after school, helping Mr Hughe

coming off drugs

Cannabis can be difficult to give up. It takes time for Alex to build up his self-confidence again and know he doesn't need the drug to help him relax or feel good about himself.

Other drugs, such as heroin, produce dramatic physical effects in people who are coming off them. These withdrawal symptoms include painful aches, cramps, sickness and shaking, which can begin only hours after the last dose. The withdrawal symptoms may last for seven to ten days.

Many countries have ways of helping people to come off drugs. Drug centres are safe places where addicts can go for advice. They may be given medicines to help them with the withdrawal symptoms. Counselling and self-help groups allow people to talk through their problems and feelings. Even so, recovering from drug addiction can take years.

with the scenery for the play.

23

At the end of term, the whole school is invited to watch the play.

When the time comes, Alex stands behind the curtains going over his lines in his head. He's terrified he'll forget something – but he's excited too. Then he steps on to the stage and the magic of the play takes him over.

When the curtains finally close, the hall is filled with the sound of clapping. The play's a great success.

Afterwards Alex sees Mina and Nathan. He's still very excited.

'It was brilliant!' he tells them. 'Everything flowed – I didn't forget a single word. I'll definitely try for a part in the next one!'

'Isn't that your dad over there talking to Mr Hughes?' asks Mina.

Alex nods. 'Mr Hughes had a chat with him and told him what a great actor I am!' he replies, winking. 'I might even go to drama school when I'm older.' Alex's eyes are shining.

'You used to say life was boring,' Nathan reminds him.

'I know,' laughs Alex. 'Now everything's changed.'

'You've changed - back

Thrill-seekers

Young people often take drugs for the thrill of it. Are you a thrill-seeker? There are other ways to get excitement, which won't damage your body and brain. Try out some of these activities:

- climb mountains, cross streams on ropes, canoe – join a young people's outdoor programme
- learn to hang-glide
- join a drama club – and perform!
- learn to ski

Cannabis and the law

Some people think the law should be changed about cannabis. They believe that adults should be allowed to smoke the drug, just as they can smoke cigarettes or drink alcohol (which are also harmful to their health). So far the government does not agree, and having and supplying cannabis is still a punishable offence.

Drugs and the law

Most countries have laws to control drugs and drug dealing. In many countries, people caught dealing are sent to prison. In the USA, Australia and the UK it is against the law to keep any illegal drug, even if you are not planning to sell it.

staying off drugs

nto the old Alex!"
says Mina, smiling.

Dance drugs

Dance drugs (like ecstasy, amphetamines and LSD) are stimulants. They can make people dance all night without a break. People who have taken these drugs may dehydrate, develop heatstroke or heat exhaustion. They could – and do – die. To stop this happening they should:

- drink a pint of non-alcoholic fluid every hour (sipping slowly, not all at once)
- eat salty peanuts or crisps to replace the salt lost through sweating
- allow their bodies to cool down every so often in another room
- never wear a hat while dancing (it keeps the heat in)

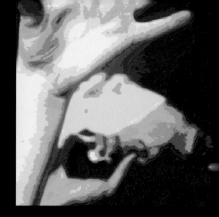

It can be hard to say no to drugs if others are taking them.

Remember, all drugs carry some kind of risk. And after every high there has to come a low. If you've decided not to take drugs, it's worth practising saying no beforehand. Here are some ways to refuse:

'No thanks, I don't do drugs.'

'No thanks, I don't need drugs to have a good time.'

'No thanks, I want to stay healthy.'

Never take drugs just to fit in with the others. Find friends who don't take drugs.

saying no to drugs

EMERGENCY!

If a friend or someone you know is in trouble through taking drugs:

- stay with him/her
- lay him/her on one side
- if the person is panicking, talk to him/her calmly
- if the person needs to be sick, lean him/her over to prevent choking
- if the person seems drowsy, try to keep him/her awake
- if the person pants and gasps for breath, try to get him/her to breathe slowly and deeply

If your friend faints or is unconscious:
- **Don't leave him/her alone**
- **Send someone to call an ambulance**
- **Get help from an adult**
- **Always tell an adult what you think your friend has taken. You won't get into trouble – and it could save your friend's life.**

If your friend loses consciousness, roll him/her over on to one side to prevent choking.

The following is a list of illegal drugs and their effects (but remember, you can never be completely sure what the effect of a drug will be).

Amphetamines
(speed, whizz, uppers)
- powder or tablets
- swallowed, sniffed, injected or smoked
- good feelings: wakefulness, energy, happiness
- bad feelings: panic, depression

Cannabis
(marijuana, grass, dope, weed, hash, pot, joints, spliffs)
- herbal grass, resin or oil
- smoked or eaten
- cannabis can be drunk in a kind of 'tea'. Taken like this, the effects last longer. High doses can cause people to become unconscious.
- good feelings: relaxation, friendliness, changes the way you see and hear things
- bad feelings: panic, fear
- long-term use may damage the part of the brain concerned with learning
- cannabis taken with alcohol can make people violent. Cannabis mixed with ecstasy or speed can make you seriously dehydrated.
- marijuana smoke contains some of the same cancer-causing chemicals as tobacco, sometimes in higher concentrations. Someone who smokes five joints a week may be taking in as many cancer-causing chemicals as someone who smokes a packet of cigarettes a day.

Cocaine
(charlie, snow, crack)
- white powder or crystals
- sniffed or smoked
- good feelings: well-being, no pain or tiredness
- bad feelings: sleeplessness, restlessness, anxiety

Ecstasy
(E, doves, disco biscuits, adam, MDMA)

- tablets
- swallowed
- good feelings: happiness, friendliness, energy
- bad feelings: sickness, tiredness, feeling low afterwards

Heroin
(smack, H, skag, junk, brown sugar)
- brown or white powder
- injected, sniffed or smoked
- good feelings: happiness, peacefulness, relaxation
- bad feelings: sickness, dizziness
- injecting drugs can damage veins. Infected needles spread disease, including AIDS.

LSD (acid, trips, blotters)
- paper squares or tablets
- swallowed
- good feelings: well being, fantastic sounds and visions, changes the way you see and hear things
- bad feelings: nightmare visions, fear; once a trip has started, it's impossible to stop it

Magic mushrooms
(shrooms, caps, mushies, psilocybin)
- dried or fresh mushrooms
  - eaten
    - good feelings: well-being, fantastic visions and sounds, changes the way you see and hear things
- bad feelings: fear, nightmare visions, sickness

Anabolic steroids
('roids)
- injected or swallowed
- these drugs are taken to improve strength and endurance and to over-develop bodies
- side effects: breasts can develop in boys and testicles can shrink; in girls, hair can grow on the face, breasts can shrink and the voice can deepen

Inhalants
- solvents, including glues, aerosols, varnishes, cleaners, paints
- inhaled
- good feelings: well-being, fantastic visions
- bad feelings: sickness, sleepiness, headaches

IT IS DANGEROUS TO:
- mix drugs (that includes alcohol) – you can't tell what the effect will be
- take any drug if you are already taking medicine (such as antibiotics, or medication for asthma or epilepsy) – mixing can change the effects of both drugs
- take another dose of a drug soon after the first one
- drive, swim, cycle, climb, run or work machinery if you have taken drugs
- get in a car with a driver who has been taking drugs

drug facts

glossary

craving a powerful longing for a drug.

dehydrate to cause a dangerous loss of water in the body.

depressant a type of drug which slows down brain activity.

flashback a side-effect of taking a hallucinogen, in which the first effects of the drug return a while later.

hallucinogen a type of drug that changes the way you see or hear things.

heat exhaustion a dangerous condition caused by being very active in extreme heat. Sufferers become dizzy, have stomach pains and may collapse.

heatstroke a dangerous condition in which the body can no longer control temperature by sweating. Sufferers have a high temperature, hot, dry skin, and may fall unconscious.

inhalants chemicals that are breathed in to give mind-changing effects. Most inhalants are solvents (liquids which can dissolve other substances) such as varnishes, paints and glues.

narcotic a drug that causes sleepiness, drowsiness and sometimes unconsciousness.

nerves tiny cords that send messages between your brain and other parts of your body.

stimulant a type of drug that speeds up brain activity, and makes the user over-energetic.

stoned affected by a drug.

synthetic drug a drug made in a laboratory.

tolerance the body's ability to cope with the effects of a drug.

trip the experience someone has after taking a hallucinogenic drug.

further information

Getting Help

If you have a problem with drugs, there are people who can help. Talk to an adult you trust. Go to your doctor. You could also phone one of the organisations listed below. Sometimes the telephone lines are busy. If they are, don't give up – keep trying.

National Drugs Helpline

Freephone 0800 77 66 00
This organisation can also put you in touch with a drugs agency near where you live.

Re-Solv

Freephone 0808 800 2345
Information and advice on solvent abuse.

ADFAM National

020 7928 8900
For friends and families of drug users.

ChildLine

Freephone 0800 1111

Websites

The following websites have information about drug-related problems:

http://www.drugsinfofile.com

ChildLine
http://www.childline.org.uk

index